CONDITIONAL MASTERY: A BEGINNER'S GUIDE TO IF-ELSE STATEMENTS IN C++, C, AND

By

Dr Issa Ngoie

Introduction

C++ is an intermediate-level language; learning this language will give you a much deeper understanding of programming structure. In C++, you have to write, declare, and explain everything in the source code, giving you a deeper knowledge of all the program parts.

Python vs. C++: Which language is better?

The Python vs. C++ duel lacks a clear winner, as the better choice **depends on individual preferences and project requirements**. Python excels in quick learning and the rapid development of small programs. In contrast, C++ is suitable for large projects and exploring multiple languages, although it requires more time to master. With influential companies like Google favoring Python and Netflix relying on C++, both languages are poised to have significant roles in the future.

Brief history of C and Python.

C was created by Dennis Ritchie at Bell Labs in the early 1970s as an augmented version of Ken Thompson's B. Another Bell Labs employee, Brian Kernighan, had written the first C tutorial, and he persuaded Ritchie to coauthor a book on the language.

Python is a widely used general-purpose, high-level programming language. It was initially designed by **Guido van Rossum in 1991** and developed by Python Software Foundation. It was mainly developed for emphasis on code readability, and its syntax allows programmers to express concepts in fewer lines of code.

An Online compiler is a tool that allows you to compile source code and run it in several different programming languages online. An online compiler is needed for program execution. It converts the text-based source code into an executable representation known as **object code**.

The link below allow you to test your C++ online without additional tools.

https://www.programiz.com/cpp-programming/online-compiler/

The link below will allow you to test your **python code** online without additional tools

https://www.programiz.com/python-programming/online-compiler/

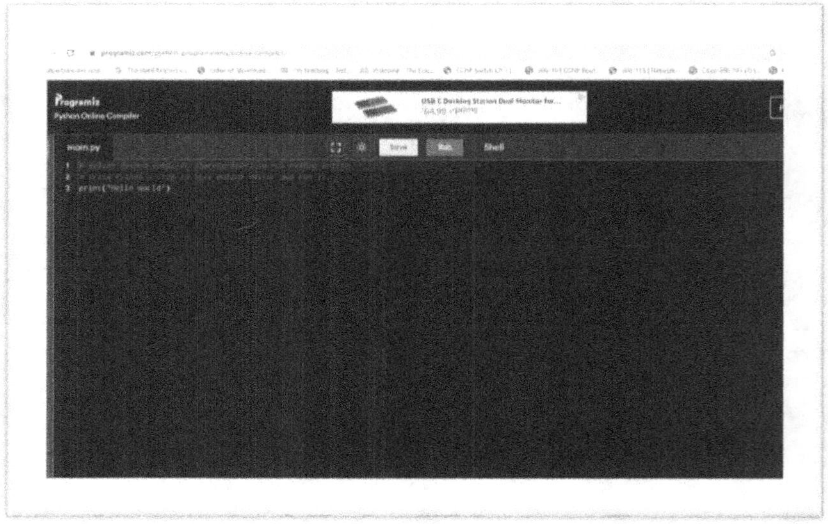

The link below will allow you to **use C online Compiler**, you need only internet connectivity

https://www.programiz.com/c-programming/online-compiler/

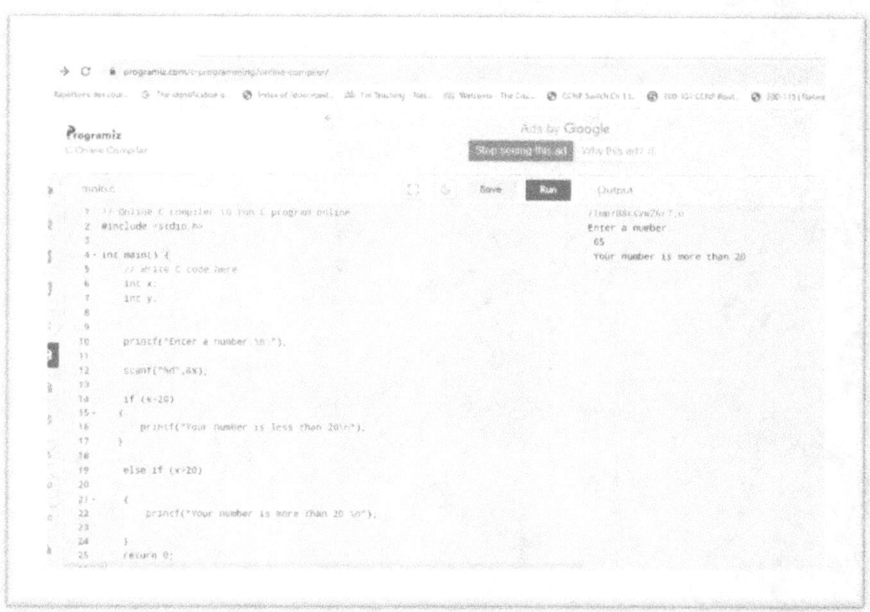

An if statement is a condition statement used to check a condition, and execute it if the condition holds true. It is also a control flow statement, which utilizes decision-making to control the flow of execution.

In C we are using parenthesis and bracket instead of semi-colon

1. Print out or display hello world message if the input from the user is less than 5.

Solution in C++

```cpp
#include <iostream>

int main() {
    int x ;

    std::cout<<"Enter a number:";
    std::cin>>x;

if (x<5) {
  std::cout << x<<" is less than y";
}

    return 0;
}
```

Output

```
Enter a number:1
1 is less than y
```

Solution in Python

```
x=int(input(("Enter a number :")))
y= "Hello World"

if x<5:
    print("Hello World")
```

```
Enter a number :3
Hello World
```

In C language

```c
2  #include <stdio.h>
3
4  int main() {
5      // Write C code here
6      int x;
7      printf("Enter a number: ");
8      scanf("%d",&x);
9
10     if  (x<5)
11
12     {
13         printf("Hello World");
14 }
15
16     return 0;
17 }
```

Output

```
Enter a number: 2
Hello World
```

2. Print out or display Hello world message three times if the user insert a number less than 10.

Solution in C++

```cpp
#include <iostream>

int main() {
    int x ;


    std::cout<<"Enter a number:";
    std::cin>>x;


if (x<10) {
  std::cout << " Hello World!\n";
    std::cout << " Hello World!\n";
  std::cout << " Hello World!\n";


}


    return 0;
}
```

Output

```
Enter a number:8
Hello World!
 Hello World!
 Hello World!
```

Solution in Python

```python
x=int(input(("Enter a number :")))
y= "Hello World"

if x<5:
    print("Hello World")
```

```
Enter a number :3
Hello World
```

```python
x=int(input(("Enter a number :")))
y= "Hello World"

if x<10:
    print("Hello World")
    print("Hello World")
    print("Hello World")
```

```
Enter a number :7
Hello World
Hello World
Hello World
```

Solution in C

```c
#include <stdio.h>

int main() {
    // Write C code here
    int x;
    printf("Enter a number: ");
    scanf("%d",&x);

    if  (x<10)

    {
        printf("Hello World\n");
          printf("Hello World\n");
            printf("Hello World\n");
}

    return 0;
}
```

3. Ask a user to insert two numbers and display the sum, product and division of those numbers.

Solution in C++

```cpp
#include <iostream>
int main() {
    int a;int b; int d;
    int s;int p;
    std::cout<<"Enter your first number:";
    std::cin>>a;
    std::cout<<"Enter your Second number:";
    std::cin>>b;
     s=a+b;
     p=a*b;
     d=a/b;
  std::cout << " The sum is: "<<s;
  std::cout << " The product is: "<<p;
  std::cout << " The division is: "<<d;



        return 0;
}
```

Output

```
Enter your first number:2
Enter your Second number:4
The sum is: 6 The product is: 8 The division is: 0
```

Solution in Python

```python
x=int(input(("Enter your first number :")))
z=int(input(("Enter your second  number :")))
s=x+z
p=x*z
d=x/z

print("The sum, the product and the division of your two numbers are",s,p,d)
```

```
Enter your first number :4
Enter your second  number :2
The sum, the product and the division of your two numbers are 6 8 2.0
```

Solution in C

Output

```c
#include <stdio.h>

int main() {
    // Write C code here
    int x;
    int y;
    int Div;
    int Sum;
    int Pro;
    printf("Enter a number:\n ");

    scanf("%d",&x);

        printf("Enter a number:\n ");

    scanf("%d",&y);

    Sum=x+y;
    Div=x/y;
    Pro=x*y;

    printf("the sum is %d, the product is %d and the division is %d", Sum,Pro,Div
    );

    return 0;
}
```

```
Enter a number:
 10
 Enter a number:
 10
 the sum is 20, the product is 100 and the division is 1
```

4. Print the sum of two numbers if both are less than 20.

Solution in C++

```cpp
#include <iostream>

int main() {
    int x;
    int y;
    int s;

    std::cout<<"Enter your first number:";
    std::cin>>x;
        std::cout<<"Enter your second number:";
    std::cin>>y;
    s=x+y;
if (x<20 && y<20) {
   std::cout << " The sum of your two numbers is: " << s ;

}

    return 0;
}
```

Output

```
Enter your first number:5
Enter your second number:3
The sum of your two numbers is: 8
```

Solution in Python

```python
x=int(input(("Enter your first number :")))
z=int(input(("Enter your second  number :")))
s=x+z

if x<20 and z<20:

    print ("The sum of your two numbers is :", s)
```

```
Enter your first number :4
Enter your second  number :6
The sum of your two numbers is : 10
```

Solution in C

```c
int main() {
    // Write C code here
    int x;
    int y;

    int Sum;

    printf("Enter a number:\n ");

    scanf("%d",&x);

        printf("Enter your second number:\n ");

     scanf("%d",&y);

     Sum=x+y;


    if (x<20 & y<20)

    {
        printf("the sum is %d", Sum);

    }
    return 0;
}
```

Output

```
Enter a number:
 15
 Enter your second number:
 18
 the sum is 33
```

5. Print out the message " Your number is less than 20" if a user inser a number less 20, and print out the message " Your number is more than 20 if the number inserted is more than 20".

Solution in C++

```cpp
#include <iostream>

int main() {
    int x;

    std::cout<<"Enter your first number:";
    std::cin>>x;

if (x<20) {
  std::cout << " The number entered is less than ·20";

}
else {
        std::cout<<"The number entered is more than 20";
    }


    return 0;
}
```

Output

```
Enter your first number:2
The number entered is less than 20
```

Solution in Python

```python
x=int(input(("Enter your first number :")))

if x<20:
    print(x,"is less than 20")


else:
     print(x,"is more than 20")
```

```
Enter your first number :7
7 is less than 20
```

Solution in C

```c
#include <stdio.h>

int main() {
    // Write C code here
    int x;
    int y;


    printf("Enter a number:\n ");

    scanf("%d",&x);

    if (x<20)
    {
        printf("Your number is less than 20\n");
    }

    else if (x>20)

    {
        printf("Your number is more than 20 \n");

    }
    return 0;
}
```

Output

```
Enter a number:
 65
Your number is more than 20
```

6. Print out the message " Your number is less
   than 20" if a user insert a number less 20, and
   print out the message " Your number is more

than 20 if the number inserted is more than 20. If the number inserted is equal to 20, print out "Number is equal to 20".

```
: x=int(input(("Enter your first number :")))

if x<20:
    print(x,"is less than 20")
elif x==20:
    print(x,"is equal to 20")

else:
     print(x,"is more than 20")
```

```
Enter your first number :30
30 is more than 20
```

7. Print out the solution of a quadratic equation with it form $ax^2+bx+c=o$ by asking a user to insert the values of a, b and c

Solution in C++

```cpp
#include <iostream>
int main() {
    int a;int b;int c; int delta;
    int s;int s1;int s2;
    std::cout<<"Enter your first number:";
    std::cin>>a;
    std::cout<<"Enter your Second number:";
    std::cin>>b;
    std::cout<<"Enter your Third number:";
    std::cin>>c;
     delta=(b^2)-(4*a*c);
    if (delta<0) {
  std::cout << " There is no racine or solution";
  }
else if(delta=0) {
    s=-b/2*a;
      std::cout<<"The Solution is double roots: " << s;
  }
    else {
     s1=(-b+delta)/2*a;
         s2=(-b+delta)/2*a;
         std::cout<<"The Solution are two distinct roots"<<s1 <<s2;
}
        return 0;
}
```

Output

```
Enter your first number:1
Enter your Second number:2
Enter your Third number:1
There is no racine or solution
```

```python
y=str(input("what is your name:"))
print(y,"I will show your how to solve a quadreatic equation")

a=int(input("Enter your a value"))
b=int(input("Enter your b value"))
c=int(input("Enter your c value"))


s=a**2+b*c+c

if s<0:
    print(s,"is negative, means there is no solution for your equation")
elif s==0:
    t=-b/2*a
    print(t,"is your double root ")
else:
    st=(-b+s**0.5)/2*a
    sr=(-b-s**0.5)/2*a
    print(st,sr,"are your two distinct roots or solutions")
```

```
what is your name:Issa
Issa I will show your how to solve a quadreatic equation
Enter your a value1
Enter your b value1
Enter your c value1
0.3660254037844386 -1.3660254037844386 are your two distinct roots or solutions
```

8. Print out the square root of a number given by a user.

```python
x=int(input("Enter a number"))
print("I will show your how to find a square root of ",x)

s=x**0.5

if s<0:
    print("there is no square root for a real negative number")
else:
    print("the square root is",s)
```

```
Enter a number4
I will show your how to find a square root of  4
the square root is 2.0
```

9. Print out the solution of a linear equation (ax+b=c)

```
print("I will show you how to solve a lineare equation of the form ax+b=c")
a=int(input("Enter a number:"))
b=int(input("Enter b number:"))
s=-b/a
print("the solution of your equation is ",s)
```

```
I will show you how to solve a lineare equation of the form ax+b=c
Enter a number:4
Enter b number:5
the solution of your equation is  -1.25
```

10. Print out the cube root of a given number by the user.

```
print("I will show you how to find the cube root of any number")
a=int(input("Enter a number that you need to find the cube root"))

cu=a**1/3
print("Your cube root is ",cu)
```

```
I will show you how to find the cube root of any number
Enter a number that you need to find the cube root9
Your cube root is  3.0
```

NOTE

For Two cases use:

Example

If a<b:

    Print ("Hello")

Else:

Print ("I failed")

For Three cases use:

Example

If x<y:

    Print ("x is less than y")

Elif x>3:

    Print ("x is more than y")

Else:

    Print ("Success")

11. Print out colors according to the user input. The program will ask user to insert a number and the program will display or print out a color associated to it.

color	Numbers
Red	1
Yellow	2
Green	3
orange	4
white	5

Solution

```
y=int(input("Enter a number: "))
l=str
r=str
o=str
g=str
w=str
if y==1:
    print("your choosen color is yellow ")
elif y==2:
    print("your choosen color is Red ")
elif y==3:
    print("your choosen color is Orange ")
elif y==4:
    print("your choosen color is Green ")
elif y==5:
    print("your choosen color is white ")
else:
    print("your choosen color is unknown")
```

```
Enter a number: 2
your choosen color is Red
```

Exercises

- If - Assign 10 to x. If x is bigger than 0, print "x is a positive number".

- If-else - Assign -50 to y. If x is bigger than 0, print "x is a positive number". Else, print "x is a negative number".

- If-elif-else - Assign 0 to z. If x is bigger than 0, print "x is a positive number".

Q1. Name the keyword which helps in writing code involves condition.
Hide Answer
Ans. if

Q2. Write the syntax of simple if statement.
Hide Answer

Ans.
```
if < Condition> :
   Execute this
```


Q3. Is there any limit of statement that can appear under an if block.
Hide Answer
Ans. No

Q4. Write a program to check whether a person is eligible for voting or not. (accept age from user)
Hide Answer
Ans.
```
age=int(input("Enter your age"))
if age >=18:
   print("Eligible for voting")
else:
   print("not eligible for voting")
```

Q5. Write a program to check whether a number entered by user is even or odd.
Hide Answer
Ans.
```
num=int(input("Enter your age"))
if num%2==0:
   print("Number is Even")
else:
   print("Number is Odd")
```

Q6. Write a program to check whether a number is divisible by 7 or not.
Hide Answer
Ans.
```
num=int(input("Enter your age"))
if num%7==0:
   print("Number is divisible")
else:
   print("Number is not divisible")
```

Q7. Write a program to display "Hello" if a number entered by user is a multiple of five , otherwise print "Bye".
Hide Answer
Ans.
```
num=int(input("Enter your age"))
if num%5==0:
   print("Hello")
else:
   print("Bye")
```

Q8. Write a program to calculate the electricity bill (accept number of unit from user) according to the following criteria :

Unit	Price
First 100 units	no charge
Next 100 units	Rs 5 per unit
After 200 units	Rs 10 per unit

(For example if input unit is 350 than total bill amount is Rs2000)

Hide Answer

Ans.

```python
amt=0
nu=int(input("Enter number of electric unit"))
if nu<=100:
    amt=0
if nu>100 and nu<=200:
    amt=(nu-100)*5
if nu>200:
    amt=500+(nu-200)*10
print("Amount to pay :",amt)
```

Q9. Write a program to display the last digit of a number.
(hint : any number % 10 will return the last digit)

Hide Answer

Ans.

```python
num=int(input("Enter any number"))
print("Last digit of number is ",num%10)
```

Python vocabulary

Here we provide a list of commonly used terms that you will most probably encounter when doing Python programming.

- **Variable** is a way of storing values into the memory of the computer by using specific names that you define.
- **Data types**

    o Integer (int) = Whole number
    o Float (float) = Decimal number
    o String (str) = Text
    o Boolean (bool) = True / False
    o List (list) = A "container" that can store any kind of values. You can create a list with square brackets e.g. [1, 2, 3, 'a', 'b', 'c'].
    o Tuple (tuple) = A similar "container" as list with a difference that you cannot update the values in a tuple. You can create a tuple with parentheses (1, 2, 3, 'a', 'b', 'c').

- **Index** number is the location of specific value stored in Python lists or tuples. The first index value of list is always **0**.
- **Script** is a dedicated document for writing Python code that you can execute. Python script files should always have the `` .py `` file extension.